AN AVEC SAMPLER
1997

Editor: Cydney Chadwick

First Edition

ISBN: 1-880713-10-1

Library of Congress Catalog Card Number: 97-73805

Grateful acknowledgment to the following recent patrons of Avec Books/Syntax Projects for the Arts, without which, *An Avec Sampler* would not have been possible: Peter Straub, Craig Watson, Marjorie Perloff, Anonymous, Harry Mathews and Catherine Bowers.

Stephen-Paul Martin's "Brain Tale" is from his collection *Not Quite Fiction,* published in July 1997 by Vatic Hum Press. Reprinted with permission.

Avec Books
P.O. Box 1059
Penngrove, CA 94951

CONTENTS

Laura Moriarty: from *The Case*   5

Chris Stroffolino: *Five Poems*   16

Laynie Browne: from *The Agency of Wind*   28

George Albon: from *Step*   34

Stephen-Paul Martin: from *Not Quite Fiction*   42

Lissa McLaughlin: *Five Stories*   46

Susan Smith Nash: *Three Stories*   53

Laura Moriarty

The Circumstances of the Poem

for Nick and Columbine

after Jay De Feo and Francesco Clemente

(A woman with books)

A blue book

"Moriarty is working on the word
dream" I hear in a cafe
A black and blue script
As a wet sky and page
Behind a history (l'histoire)
An ensemble or assertion.

Watering the lawn later makes
A prism so that additional
Colors exist mostly in the range
Of yellow as in the yellow page
Of print temporarily preserved.
Or as in tempera the dream
Of painting in eggs and gold on old

Paper or other sacred surface
To form a book or wall
Like an afternoon plain blue sky or
Fabric. A girl wraps herself in it.
(The thought of cloth and wrapping)
To be draped: many girls
Similarly wrapped laugh as the room
Is entered by oneself. An added line

Or question is included to enact
The fact of addition as growth
Which becomes almost a metaphor
Or a report unlike the story
So far made of science terms like
Phenomenon, cancer, or taxonomic,
Exploratory surgery. A map is pictured
Upside down made of a hand.
Assorted body parts stenciled
On leather like stars.

But growth is unpredictable.
And body language can be translated.
It's my fault I say handing you
My head in an articulate gesture.
And you ask if this is just one of my
Projects by ripping open your chest
And then something else is added.
I hear the change in the music

Read of the birth of a child. Become awake
In spite of it's being night
And watch flowers get darker stiffly
And the days shorter by one
A girl sleeps inconsolably dreams
In Emily Dickinson white.
Restless neighbors discuss sex and the play
Is indefinite or infinite in its
Ending and someone not in this picture
Is not in this house.

But there is agreement. It is mine
To accept absence and perplexity
As if there were no substitute for anything.
"It is relaxing to be in the main room."
I enter the changes. There is no
Project in that sense and the longer
Nights are correct and the rust
Magenta and purple of those stalks
Visible even from here.

There is a lot to read and memorize.
There is a new language.
It is fall. Sleep is out of the question.
And Columbine can't remember what verbs are.
She knows one when she sees one.
We actually argue about verbs and nouns.
The house shakes me awake and the swelling
Sound of trains takes the place of foghorns.
I can't possibly be awake now.

The sky is saturated with smoke
And pigment. Thinking makes
A book of blue squares demonstrates
Thalo and aquamarine and
Overlays an unkept diary in which
Entries are pictured but not entered.
I almost make them as myself
As unkept or released.
Unkempt as the attempt becomes next
A physical idea only if

A book soaked in paint or burnt
Or dreamt as a backdrop to a scene.
French blue it is called as the cast
Of violet in Nick's face also the hue
Immediately under a certain moon
In fire season. In a book.

The immemorable is identified with language
Are the dead then language and if so
Why can they not speak? This not
Speaking these languid eyes now burnt
Also enter. The room is a furnace
Where there is sight but no eyes.
No dreamed essence even in the tangible
Things which read as the present only.
It's a threshold problem I've always said.

The blank book

The calendar is a book about books.
A white sky on a certain morning.
An uncertain morning extends in all
Directions. There's a roar in the distance
Of motion as full and always open
The freeway, the dregs of the bay and
The Golden Gate directly opposite.
A peninsular wasteland by the racetrack
Will be reclaimed as a park and the book
I'm making will be buried or burnt there
With concrete and iron broken
Things possibly plastic certainly toxic.

But then language is shown to be
A number of these same things.
As anyone in a room in a mile-square
Town might know given the silence,
Which is to say almost never.
The sun seen from one's kid's classroom
On the edge of town huge over the freeway
Setting and the waterfowl, horsestalls
Mud, tidal scum, and signs,
Bigger than the sun, make this an open
Landscape. A set of directions. A first
Language situation so transparent as to be
Invisible and quickly gone through.

And when again morning this time
Bright already the light orange changing
To yellow and white. The radio of
Drunken neighbors not quite intelligible.
(There is no news.) This day is like the next.
Except the fire danger always high.
The wind and heat and wind.
We in the West on this threshold
Of a future scene
Retrofitting the past
"The bridge has collapsed" we write.
The old futurity of the old Enlightenment
Doesn't read the same or reads exactly the same
As when Blake and Goya
Arms raised in horror or supplication
Made words out of acid and stone

Painted on the walls of the same Empire.
Insofar as those walls are inescapable
They collapse around entities drawn
To resemble ourselves watching the triumph
Back then of something like capitalism already
And now playing out each war
Famine and catastrophe.
So that this morning is of a blank wall.
The day's events change the chemistry.
They are the result of an equation
In which things are equal to one. And there is
No connection because no difference.
In a community without characteristics
The things surrounding us and us
As a thing overwhelm perception

The red book

Until the fire is inside it's autumn
And night. Someone teaches Blake in a snowstorm
In a country on the brink of civil war.
In a book about emptiness the empty points
Coalesce into stanzas and chapters.
It's an hilarious book and pointless
Or better unresolved or dissolved
And red. Redness absorbed into
The text which appears upside down
On the paper as it is dipped into an imaginary
Vat of red: not blood or paint
Not the rosé you drink for its color
But a lighter shade of dark red.
The couch of the Countess of Alba.
Strangely white and open.
Someone dying watches her eyes.

The guy next door dies. He falls
Asleep and out of his house and becomes
A statue and some photographs a wreath
Of leaves, and evokes a greenness
Into the autumn. And doesn't live
To see the yellowing of the coin tree
On his street. Or Halloween
Day after tomorrow. The clocks change
Tonight in fact now.

Emptiness is something that happens.
As we rest inside the verb we make
A fire though it's day but it's cold.
Tea and apples, bread.
A meal endlessly unfolding though eaten
In minutes. Fresh irises. Albany Island:
Columbine's title. A paper project.
A "household or city." A learning
To speak again in an angry dream or
Book of scenes from the capitol:

"Bless these elements! Their nature and use
Connect me to this place (The Capitol) its history
Temple bell rings (No Self. No Permanence.)"
(Philip Whalen) But mist changes
Early morning this view and haze brightly
Later also obscures both the attached
And cast shadows until it's mainly
A gilded lack of distinctness that distinguishes
The scene arriving home or waking there (here).
Fire burns as if frozen in place.

The word dream is this history
Late afternoon five minutes'
Quiet leaves the imprint of sun
(New season) on the same wall

portrait (forgetting)

June 22, 1996

He is no other than myself
Yet I am not now him

But electrons (he is) the medium
Stills transferred and made

To dissolve. Or otherwise
Broken. The project is not

Memory. Is impossible
The essential quality

Isn't there in the center
Where framed incompletely

Content transferred to another
". . .think of words without paper." she said.

Format as for example
Still photo or still born

"Born" he wrote on the calendar
And forty-six later (years or days)

Not unborn like done or undone
Not raw or cooked

Not nothing unreal but
Present while present "I want"

He said "to live!" in the inland
Sea where later the ashes and story

Totality and infinity and wings
Of a white insect fill the space

A tin shack shakes in the wind
There is a forest next door

Squirrels and raccoons where neighbors
Children and other agents of change

Are industrious on our behalf altering
With a wooden figure the same

Picture of oneself holding a picture
the figure gestures or sits quietly

The incense is like sage there are
Violet flowers in the thyme

It is heaven here and there
Also in that ended instance of being

Entire. Life wasted on the living
While the tea eventually becomes

The same temperature as the sea
An animal wanders in unaware

That one is human an egret
Trails shaking legs long

Rootless as he or was it I described
The ephemera left behind the wings

In jars or now flitting from mint
To bay to sorrel a swallowtail

Floats dipping seems to fall and
is (first day of summer)

Gone. Returns against
Expectations. Is gone again and

Again a sentient thing teaches
The law. It's windy at the lake

The yard collapses into many squares
Another creature like paper is taken up

Chris Stroffolino

Five Poems

Professions of Faith

Community may be a bridge from one to another
and the bridge may serve no function.
The water might as well be dry when swimming is walking
and part of me is further away from me
than you will ever be (except in thought,
the disenchantment which is *not* detachment)
To see a queen in every pawn, to love the mediators
more than the goal may be unnecessary entanglement,
a waste of time and breath. Go ahead, betray your
half-assed desire for what can't happen later
if it doesn't happen now. If now were the time for
clandestine meetings under cover of death, sensuality
would smother the love that's nothing to it, the love
that cannot care what I, or any body, thinks of it;
a jar in Tennessee that could be taken for
a new born babe with wild wolves all around it.

I go on peaceably, in a kind of defiance
with a stick up my butt. No, that's the figure
in the painting I can only see my reflection in
when blotting and being blotted before the paint dries.
The paint never dries. This is the history of the present
divvied up among a couple quarreling in doggerel
about the fate of their daughter who becomes the freedom
of the sun enforcing the norms of a subculture
I'm proud to claim as present when I take my place
at the podium just to get your goat. You see, we're already hooked;
try as I might to wriggle out from under the burden of immortality.

It's no boast to say in words that all is words.
Yet equivocation must spare at least the value of
friendship. I had to go very far into the slums of
vagueness and reputation to drown out the voices of
the dead I thought were living threats.
The decorative pursued me like a harness and
even to recount it is to count on it as a kind of crutch
that's kindling for the fire of the present that is the community
in which an atom is always split in two
in order for some me to get to some you.

The Verdict

I pray to be rid of a passing pomposity
to make way for a more permanent presumption
from the wound we would give ourselves
to fill the one we gave each other
as the desire to control silently fights
the desire to know—
the absolute zero of garden variety ghosts. . . .
the universe a snubbing thumb!
The past lies dead, as if distorted, a photo
in a scrapbook memory revises in a darkroom
not unlike the cover under which we fucked
if foreplay can be considered fucking
for when we'd throw the covers away
as if nakedness is nothing but orgasm
memories are so many there seems to be none
and before they fade there may yet be
a supernova as if it's not September
but early April in July
so we do unto others what experience
does to the meanings of words once sugared
on hilltops, steeples and billboards
to spread a blanket for the dawn
that promises nothing for solitude
but time's broad brushstrokes
presumptuous as a mouth we put words in

until the mouth becomes a word
not oblivious to the throw away society
ineluctable even to lovers in their loud laments
read as a luscious secret by young rebels
or misfits (the verdict's not in) en route
to more fleshed out articulation

of pain and what it pretends to prevent
as if a painter so drunk on possibility
he can no longer renounce realism
with a straight face in the clouds
without admitting the deformity
whose shallowness has discovered
what eluded all our wisdoms.

Moshpit

The hypothetical seems unconfined only when
all the swamps who thought they were individuals
and all the stickfigures who thought they were
a community meet in the moshpit, trade bodies
and roll out the red carpet for a past the future
will treat better than words can wield—
rushing to the unfinished finish line of once
and for all death which it thinks is sex or
other four letter riches, red letter doves,
black holes on the balkanized calendar that is a city
in the mind that contains everything in being nothing
but loose ends that need no maintenance like clothes
or like the self that is a pet that keeps you more than
you keep it, that keeps you as an "it," not an ID per se,
chained to the chessboard that doesn't have to be
a moshpit to make you sweat in society like a resume
you could pad since property is theft anyway and angels
the only solidity that resist the microscope's verdict
of spinelessness the more strongly it is churned
into jello by its own ambivalent desires for annihilation
in suburbs of fatness, of city fathers on the left bank
or rivers that wouldn't be androgynous were it not for
bridges one has to pay a toll to cross and only crosses
because money is burning a hole in the pocket of
the sunday best it refuses to ruin by swimming
in a moment that isn't neatly and conveniently
split into self and deferred other by bridgework
built to widen the difference which is fine with me
even if you don't also recognize the level
in which it's all inside a swelling you and the movie in
the lyric whose personified body parts do not have to be

organized hierarchically to mimic society unless life or
death decisions can be so central one could respond in
casual urgency to the mistaken values fear of the faith
that is "mainstream" perception once sanctified
as thought as art as war in form's hollow cut throat vote.

Singlespeak of a Double Self

Forgotten implements of jealousy disguised as desire
return as ghosts that apologize for constructing my identity
as if change is possible, though not in any once and for all sense.
Insofar as lessons go, I've learned a few, like waking one day
to realize you've never been used by treachery
as long as we begin with a negation of drama that is
a place, a clearing fog, the impossible observing
the possible some call experience
as if the past sticks like burrs to the skin
like the story of inherited sin that explains mortality
while at the same time blaming women for cheating
on us with the Adam who nicknames us snakes.
So neat, it needs to be erased.
Speaking for the spirit of negation until it too
seems the very semblance of a livable *position*
if not, per se, any self but a molten core
that might as well be breath be ice
on the runway of time as if each moment is
a departure and an arrival of a deserted plane
that seems a terrible waste to the hurry imagined conclusion
in the cemetery too slippery to be sanctified as a proper fall.
So every utopia repulses your public goodbye gifts
and hopes of return which create a space in which to cram
all the consolation prizes you've been secretly
trying to sell to others you'd dress up as your self
so as to throw them off the track of how deeply
laws of supply and demand have paralyzed
the government of emotions that can no longer
distinguish between us but in a kind of mercy
seen as a cop-out to the relentless
until relentlessness is exposed as play

and the rhetoric of science squirrel bait
and the fuckers who speak of rabbits, horses,
parrots and spaniels against the silence of
the lambs of love patch the empty body of persuasion
with fragments whose meanings play tricks
on me perhaps a tad bit more than you
who wait at the end that is happening as we speak
unless I can figure out the dead we will have become.

Party-Line Graffiti

The self-proclaimed cripple loses her case
When the defense shows a videotape of her
Wrestling in coleslaw. A mind made out of
Maxims refuses to relent, to air out
The body, or wash it in hunger.
You don't want to be cruel to the uprooted trees
You may share your bed with.
They have feelings too and just because
You cannot sing in tune with them
Is no reason to make a scene or break
A few dishes by singing a note so high
No human can hear it directly.
It is a note of joy, back when it was
Called the blues. It is the missing link
Edited out of every version of
The music of the spheres but those
Sung by dogs who have to drop a bone
To prick up their ears and shed
Their winter fur. Can we hear them
If we can't hear what they hear?

Can the full cry of the doctoral student
With the waggily tail still be heard
Amid the laughtrack of repression,
Holding onto dear life, disciples of winter,
As rodents emerge in the shadows of its dinosaur?
Revolutionaries asking us if we want a ride.
We do, of course, but from them?
What about our reputation?
What's love got to do with it?
Wouldn't it be simpler if we could meet halfway,

If I didn't have to snowshoe over the Rockies
To get to you and find you've gone to hike
The more casual sedentary mountains
That are my habitual fictive backdrop?
Is it possible that no one called it a great divide
Until a golden spike was driven in
And freedom would not ring were not the bell cracked
And the "linty" flaws for which we stand
Become too easily sacred and I am scared
I trample on the memory you tremble.

Times like these when I wanna stalk
The superficial desires I doubt I can act on
Rather than the deeper ones I can
Only act on by doubting. I do not doubt
These desires. I only doubt that they are doubt
As a gap expands to be traversed by triggers
Firing bang flags which used to be as attractive
As nostalgia for the moist city surrounding me
Like a tongue reminding me of a grandmother
Gathering dandelions beneath the Brooklyn Bridge
For the soup of simplicity that gets
The last word on my attention deficit syndrome
Which is more easily condemned than killed.

How flattering, too, the photograph in which I am
A spider somersaulting into the jaws of his mate,
Or the one of us digging a garden and not counting
On any tomatoes or tomorrows in a world
Where we can only live hand to mouth which is
So easy to forget in a world of loans and savings
And ceilings that have to be looked at askew
To start snowing on my sofa! How flattering
To be pictured setting fire to every TV in town
(in hopes of being televised). And spending
My last good dollar on a wallet, I won my case

But lost it again in the kiln only a perverse clay
Would consent to be put in without the promise
Of eventual cooling. That may be how it started.
But in the oven the promises melt. Reason may
Airbrush the oven from the photograph
But the photos, too, get thrown into the oven
Of our lovin' that cannot speak but if it could
It would surely call reason treason for condemning
The gentleness only possible in lust
To the fast lane or fast track or flippered race
Up the stairs of the waterslide of conscious personality
The reruns of the rainbow may ravish more savagely
In boy meets girl cranberry *chalance.*

A stillness seems to slow down,
Present division sees past manyness as one
In the rearview mirror never shattered enough,
Never off enough to be on. It was a thrill to strip
For the blind woman, to let ghosts fondle me and
Stencil Party Line Graffiti on every straightforward
Hearse harpooned into the waiting room, lassoed
By a once in a lifetime high-school, and be plopped
Like a tornado into a hospital at amazement
At my own solidity, a flipside not played
Until the sea recedes and the bicyclists arrive
Before the motorists to the senses seen as censors
To those with saunas they wish to proffer
As thick (political) skins.

What others regard as my virtues I no longer regard virtuously
Until the Honda I've never seen (yours)
Pulls into the interstate driveway of my thoughts
And lets me commit more crimes of desire
As if I am a priest blessing the house and demanding
The money you wouldn't know what to do with

Without me. The blessing goes something like this:
"What good is the flag that signifies freedom
if you can't burn it? What good is democracy
if we can't all be tyrants? What good is a castle
unless it's made of sex? And what good is sex
if it's not a form of tribute, a structure that can be sold,
but, if felt intensely, could eventually sell away the store?"

Nothing can hold you, even abstractions would whine
Were they not too busy cancelling each other out
To lead my tongue to your eyebrow and telling it
Not to lick, as if acknowledged cruelty is easier
To manage than the frightened floaters we become
In floods of money paving the future with fragments
To clog up the flow. Passion is play's only populists
And delight only becomes terror to ward off the filth
Of philosophy, the mischief of belief, from the land
Of laughter and forgiveness I need more faith in
Like I need a hole in my head. If we can meet in the oven
Where palaces are tenements, each flick of fortune's finger
May roll a fling around us like a red carpet to crown the sea
Without killing it by establishing pure madcap sex zones
Between the embarrassed world trade tower legs
Of an ex who wanted to dance on my nose.
(But I guess I'll carry on, even if you fail to call my bluff.)

Laynie Browne

FROM THE AGENCY OF WIND

The Bank of Common Knowledge

I began to compose a letter in my head. It began,
'dear squirrel,' but I was interrupted by the
woman who called me "dear." She was saying,

We work by basis of contribution, and drawing
upon the common bank. In order to begin, you
must first make a deposit. Our minimum is one
hundred. I looked up and saw a sign above my
head.

The Bank of Common Knowledge

She said, there is also the small matter of fees. I
had no money, but since she said it was a "small"
matter I decided to say nothing. Alright, I said,
may I have some paper, and I will begin. I sat in
a corner at a small table with a miniature pencil,
next to a female alligator who appeared to be
flustered. She kept sighing and panting, and
sliding her scales on her table which made a

most unpleasant noise. I tried to ignore her, although I could not help but to sympathize with her predicament. My list began with the following:

It is common knowledge that many living things require no door, nor doorstep.

It is common knowledge that many living things require no guardian, nor distinguishing characteristics.

It is common knowledge that the wind has no door.

It is common knowledge that windmills are actually persons with very strong arms.

It is common knowledge that this alligator beside me is having difficulties.

It is common knowledge that questions cannot be left behind; they cling most unkindly, but as they are innocent as children, one must take them along.

I had gotten this far when the alligator beside me got up noisily and lumbered away, knocking this and that with her tail as she went. She must have stuck her snout over my shoulder and was reading my list when she came to item five, and took it personally. I did feel annoyed, since those with snouts really shouldn't snoop. I was just adding this to my list:

It is common knowledge that those with snouts really shouldn't snoop.

when the "dear" lady came over to see what progress I was making. Her face made a variety of expressions while she read so that it was difficult to tell whether she was pleased.

Well, she began, I am personally much obliged to you for encouraging Alexandra to leave us.

Alexandra, I asked.

Yes, the alligator. You see, we find it most inappropriate to house reptiles.

But why, I asked, discriminate on the basis of blood temperature?

We are much indebted to you, she replied, ignoring my question, and on this basis we will accept your application. You need go no further.

Her cruelty was simply too much to bear. I thought of Alexandra and stood to leave, but then I decided to make an inquiry first, and resumed my seat.

I am most interested to know, has a crane passed this way recently, or a doormaker?

Certainly not!

Just then the walls began to creak, as if a storm were approaching. I could have sworn I saw the distinct outline of a crab within her right pupil.

Perhaps the wind has kept them away, I wondered aloud. At this comment of mine, her complexion noticeably colored.

She spoke in some temper: It is common knowledge that the wind is a very impatient and flighty entity. The last time the wind came through our office it took us quite some time to recover.

I was taken aback by the change in her manner. She looked around herself at the voluminous books fastened upon the walls with claws. It became clear that she had been all the while attempting to compose her features, searching for an appropriate thing to say. When she had accomplished her task she returned her gaze to me and spoke again.

I'm sorry, she replied, but we cannot accept your application.

Knowing my place exactly, and what I must do, I answered with all the seriousness I could summon:

That is most unfortunate, since I am not at present accepting refusals.

She made no reply. Her crab pupil scuttered, as if to follow me to the door. But she hastily closed her lid and clasped her hand over it firmly.

As I walked away the bank seemed to gleam like one copper coin being dropped. The sight was so clear in my mind I had but to turn around just in time to see a pig who was so large, that its hoof could easily hold the entire bank of common knowledge. The pig lifted the bank, looked quickly around, and then swiftly dropped it through a large slit in its back. This accomplished, the pig ran into the distance, creating a large amount of dust as it went. The last I saw was the flourish of its curly tail at the horizon. The ground was shaking. I sat down to recover my balance. I thought of the "dear" woman. No doubt she would not have many applicants to turn away now. Thank goodness Alexandra and I had not remained within its premises. There was a big crack in the earth in front of me that must have opened up during the giant pig's departure. I was still clutching my list of items of common knowledge

It is common knowledge that the "dear" woman was never "dear."

I threw the list into the crack and rose to my knees.

George Albon

to be reminded
of the failing
mainspring

not the sudden silence
but the relative
after human shout

a grimace told
him to take the
lever farther

the yet green used
marks a tongues
-width to tally

a different sound
preceded every word
—slowth of the term

to feel hips
as if new tangents
were bolting

iridescence as old
story, that brought
cold from deep

a will moves into
an upper chamber
among rival unknowns

declension toward one
end—the merest
light-sensitive dot

a perfect world
the strokes same light value
runny, evened

illuminations came
from the plant
the signal set

search for asylum
carried on in an
inner distortion

a perfect world
a trail widens out the
code of indents

channels serving
both prey and
interpreters

arms back, re-
laxed nerves as
in a vat

a perfect world
placed hand on
the breathing field

the choices are circled
until so dark they
must be chosen over

someone in estranged
weather passed past
"these doors don't"

a perfect world
living manifests of
nipple or tip

worked back into
the locus one had
thought delivered

rectangles seep with
the slight growing, to
walk out onto them

a perfect world
the identities
traced above a ground

print as enlarged
location, geographies
of the whorl

the smile that held
no life but an erect
ransom-shadow

a perfect world,
fingerpoint
out past the plain

the hymn breaks down
and space shines through,
space shines through

we to be bound
as artless they who
stead the margin

face of the world
in a man's face
moving on his front

heard in the mind,
i.e., unauditioned
as long twos

blow-ones lean
against the tap- and
beat-ones, the signings

not waiting, but
emerges as Nature
to the true situation

not one after the
next but offered
pieces in a circle

placement hardens
into act, a past-
less fact

raining, to feel
cover—us, the
locally fallen

algae, icons, in
hand's lengths, one
floating, one sunk

spoke intentions
to involving murmur
as bare murmur

held the float so
turns this and that—
limbs clenched

walking through happen-
ing, angles for tones
to deepen to leave

the perimeter of various
means stalked without
reason, without reason

the oppressor's heri-
tage—ducted into
the curb scape

before the Mister-face
coming up on a
deflect-language

shield symbols but
still the determi-
nation to mass "round"

in the afternoon
being all were all
one and self

for what is at post
the message-author
is simply "one"

image as quarry
the walking disparate
quarry as image

firster here/there
leach then gets lift
(what remains)

weight, and then
an outrance making
weight light

spun in all di-
rections—a constants
of unlocation

Stephen-Paul Martin

FROM Not Quite Fiction

Brain Tale

Janet wanted Bobby's head. It felt like a matter of life and death. Her thoughts were good, she thought, but not good enough. She needed Bobby's thoughts. She thought his thoughts were the best, and only the best would survive in the long run. She wasn't sure what the long run was, but it filled her with a nameless dread. She gave it a name but the name itself became a nameless dread. She kept on giving it names but each became a nameless dread. She needed Bobby's thoughts. She needed everything he felt and said. She waited until he was looking the other way. Then she cut off his head.

She waited until the blood was gone. Then she cut through the bone straight into the brain. It made the noise of a serial killer drilling out of jail, or masochistic lovers going wild on a bed of nails. She planned to spoon his thoughts out into a jar she kept in the john, change them into a code of zeroes and ones in a special sequence, run them through a computer simulating their chemical structure, something she could reproduce in the lab she'd built in the cellar, a liquid substance Janet would either drink or inject in her veins.

But his thoughts weren't in his brain. She looked on the top and she looked on the bottom, carefully probed with a fork and a spoon, tried her mother's tweezers. She paused and tried to think of herself as calm and clear, objective. But adjectives had never done her much good. They were too subjective. They opened the door for questions built like rooms with disappearing floors. Maybe his thoughts had never made their homes in the folds of his brain, or maybe death had cancelled them out, or maybe they'd flown away to join all other disembodied thoughts, or maybe they had no independent existence. Maybe they'd never been anything but a method of organization, a means of making a world from all those things outside his head. But none of these possibilities stayed in place for more than the blink of an eye. They didn't amount to a whole lot more than a missing twelve on a grandfather clock, though each was like a mild electric shock or a crease in the sky.

She searched in every crease of his trembling brain but there wasn't a single thought. She found instead a periscope, a telescope, a microscope, a microchip comprised of the clicks of a lock and the ticks of a clock, a small mid-American town called Hope, a time bomb on a dock, a Gothic mansion bought with dollars made by selling dope, a fancy menu offering a meal of morning shadows, gliding on the walls of a mansion just outside a town called Hope, the President in a small dark room, dangling from a rope. Janet ripped off a piece of the brain and stuffed it in her mouth. It tasted like the cheese of a pizza heaped up into a steaming ball, a sphere of convolutions making the planet look like a midnight snack, billions of neural connections making themselves look scientific.

Suddenly she recoiled in fear. The brain was becoming a message, and even worse, a task. It was telling her where to go and what to do, sending her on a quest, a journey west of the sun and east of the moon, to find by any means possible the reason life is so unfair, to accept that reason itself as being logical and fair, framed in a sentence so perfectly made, so carefully pitched and balanced, that no one could possibly say what it meant or speculate on its origins, words comprised of syllables consuming all description, all careful accounts that went by the comic name of interpretation. The sentence would include all things but make a hole in the sum of their parts. Reading it would be like reading nothing fifteen billion times. Things would be suddenly different. She wouldn't have moods anymore. Her time would be spent in a place where slowing down was just like speeding up, where faces could be changed by typing letters on a keyboard.

She'd have to drop the mask of pain and face the mask of chaos, the mask of order in chaos, order made in the shape of chaos, and not live out the rest of her life resenting a more-than-human force, a bad-ass white-haired prick in the sky, a vast abbreviation, an absolute brute principle that never gave her what she deserved, what everyone she knew agreed she deserved. The task was obnoxious. It made her sick to her stomach, made her want to become anorexic, throw tantrums up and down the banks of slow polluted rivers. The moment got consumed in topological distortions, forcing time to cluster into an alphabet of regret, as if she'd left her name in Illinois or Minnesota, or someone else had left an old gray mare in place of her mother's car, a Babylonian almanac in place of her sister's bass guitar, a yellow such and a red because in place of her brother's cheap cigars. The task was more than obnoxious; it was outrageous. The task was more than adjectives that seem to be contagious. After all, if she couldn't blame the universe, who could she blame? Herself?

She didn't think so. She knew that if she blamed herself she'd brutalize herself, cut herself into four distinct personalities, four phantom selves, each of which would claim to be the only one, her central self. One of them would be nice all the time, doing things for others, never making anything of herself, an under-achiever, making herself a reflection of those whose anger she'd abducted. Another personality would be the take-charge type, feeling entitled to boss her friends around, control their decisions, manipulate their emotions, turn their molehills into mountains. Yet another self would be consumed in a mythic past, sifting obsessively through her childhood pain, constructing a story, calling it self-awareness, calling it healing herself in a patient way, never calling it boring self-defeating self-absorption. Her fourth sub-personality would be a drunk or an acid head, lost in a pseudo-Dionysian quest for a self beyond the self, a non-first-person subjectivity not comprised of goals and a past, not organized around three meals a day, four standard seasons, not built by nouns directing verbs, not built on rules and reasons.

The very thought of becoming multiple filled her veins with old Scotch tape. She couldn't afford to blame anymore, not any one or any thing, and certainly not herself. But what would life be like without blaming? Would it be like dropping a hundred pounds in a week or on the floor? Or like an appliance made from bad mistakes in long division? A plastic model of a great white shark to play with in a bathtub? A prostitute who keeps a three-star general on a leash? She warned herself she better not try to find out, but she had to find out. She warned herself again, but she had to find out. She warned herself again. The word again became a nameless dread, the tick of a clock in her head. She thought of turning away in fear with moody soundtrack music. But she couldn't escape the chunk of ice in her belly. She couldn't escape the wounded horse of metaphor in her groin. She stared at the brain for more than twenty-nine minutes, thirty-three seconds. Bobby's brain was blue at first, then green and yellow-green, yellow turning white, white like a sky with black stars twinkling. She thought it might explode, a white dwarf star, a super nova, sending light-years into the dark of time in every direction.

She turned her face away from the brain and tried to face the quest. Exactly what would it be? She thought she knew. It made her nauseous. She knew that she would confront obnoxious obstacles, ordeals, monsters trapped in syntax, in rocks and clouds and the green of grass, trapped in the see-through space of glass, on blackboards after class, on beaches when she tried to relax, on football teams that came in last. It was all spelled out in the convolutions Janet knew as Bobby's brain, spelled in the same way monkeys type accidental words on keyboards. She knew in advance of course that the end would try to seem unforeseen, leaving her in the sudden shape of a jagged seaside cliff, rock formations people read as alphabets of regret. They'd stare entranced for centuries at the face of a coded message, telling themselves mythological tales to account for the text of stone, sagas based on Janet's need for thoughts that weren't her own.

The brain kept getting bigger as it filled itself with provisional space, the only way to keep from becoming a fish in a partially frozen bay, a dolphin shaped as a cloud above that bay in the cool of the day, a dog whose barking destroys an outdoor violin concerto, an opera singer getting mad and crumpling a libretto, a virus disguised as a frog that crashes the Pentagon's computers, a party where people wear name-tags and take each other's pictures, a calendar with a painting of the moon above a tramp steamer, a city of more than fifteen million oppressively cheerful people, an observation balloon that pops itself on a Gothic steeple, a sunrise made of psychedelic drugs, a brick in a bathtub, a hall of floor-length mirrors misting over at four in the morning, a wedding invitation made to sound more like a warning, a saw coming up through floorboards cutting a circle around the President's feet, a beer commercial filled with jocks who've never known defeat, a musical score comprised of bricks and lightbulbs in a blender, a werewolf waking up each day in the bed of a public defender, someone who thinks that people who fart in church are self-destructive, someone who thinks that Miss America pageants are repulsive, someone who thinks the machinery of time is non-discursive, someone who thinks that opening someone's head is too intrusive.

Janet began to feel guilt. She'd been a bad girl. Now Bobby was dead. She never should have cut his head in half while he was still alive. Now she'd lost her only friend, the best one that she'd ever had. There was only one thing to do—begin her quest. She packed her belongings, which now included everything she'd found in Bobby's head.

Lissa McLaughlin

FIVE STORIES

California

for Keith Waldrop

I love Richard Nixon, says my mother. What a beautiful man. She has that book of Nixon's sayings, it's small, thin, but she holds it with both hands. I've got him under my skin. That's gross, Ma, I say. She socks my head, pulls my head over and kisses it. Look, she says, as a baby Richard was tiny growing up in California. His mother was strict, but she was fair. There, my mother points, the manly jaw.

My father shakes his head. She's a stubborn son of a bitch, your mother. Right after that bad business at the doctor's she got on this Nixon thing. I'd like to kill that guy, too bad he's dead. Remember Rudy's musical saw recital, everyone from the church came? Your mother took it into her head to show slides. The Nixon family sidewalk. Dick's first marble. Rudy bent his saw almost in half trying to keep up. One more time, she told him, Hail to the Chief. She helped everyone on with their coats, how can I forget? You don't have to, they said at the door, watching her hands on their buttons.

My mother keeps Nixon's sayings by her bedside table. She says they're there if the news on TV is bad, hollow, no moral fiber. Don't lose my place, she orders. She grabs me, Listen to this one, but it's the same speech over and over. The Communists somewhere waiting, dark immigrants pooling over California, something is dripping, something else is being sipped, cruelly, inward. Sometimes on my way to piss there's nothing else except the pine tree scrubbing the house, and I hear her in there reading, "This whole world's getting later."

One day I bring Jim home from the plant. We make those machines that blow insulation into walls, a small operation, a family-run business. Jim's father owns it. My mother met his father at a Nixon rally. He has this tattoo, "Hats Off to Dick Nixon." He can't come to the house because my father would like to blow his head off. Away from the plant Jim stops talking about Nixon, or insulation. We laugh about which is more nuts, my mother or his father. My mother loves Jim, who reminds her of Jim's father who is forbidden to drive up the driveway. You boys must be starving, she says when she comes out of the kitchen, her face wet with sweat. Just wait, I tell Jim. My mother brings in French fries. Where's the ketchup? says Jim. There is none, says my mother. But Nixon put it on everything, he says. Impossible, she says, ketchup is disgusting. She watches us eat without touching anything. I can tell about you, Jim. What? Jim says. Jim, you're a Nixon man.

There's that bird sitting, scratching its head, lifting one leg like it's a dog. Take that bird out of here, my mother says, that red thing. She doesn't like anything red. Drop dead, she calls out through the curtains, creeping around. Not cherries. Not cardinals. Ketchup in restaurants so stiff it's almost black.

For years she hasn't eaten. I can't, she says. I can't, or I might choke. Like that bird, moving the pine needles against its mouth. Her friend got lost that way, at the doctor's. My mother wasn't there, but she told me. Her friend was allergic and her face went black. By then it was too late. I did it, says my mother. Evelyn, her only friend. A feeling watered down, sloshing, spilling out.

And still it gets later. I lie awake and I can't stop thinking of my work. Insulation. A sucker instead of a nozzle, pulling me in. My mother and her friend. My father who taught me to drink. He goes to bed before she does. In this bad light a hand gets to looking funny, everything does. And I ask myself, What makes this a hand, the crud under my nails? That light around my fingers?

It's night, and I knock on her door. On TV I've been watching wrestling. Read this, she says, and hands me Nixon's sayings. It's the same speech it always is, but I think I'll start. Then a picture falls out. My mother's still young, newly married. She's in a coat with a fur collar, and there's another woman, same collar. They don't even need to look at each other. My mother holds the picture smiling. It was just a shot, she says, at his office. Ma, I say, but she pushes me away. And there's Evelyn laughing, Drop dead. Laughing, with her black tongue, You're late, like you always are.

I imagine meeting Nixon. He has that 5 o'clock shadow and I have to work not to laugh. My mother would love it, me and Dick at last. Now he lifts one hand and something happens near his mouth. Dick, what is it? I call. Something got you down? Nixon's grinning now, and his fingers take my arm. They push downward, all at once. Then one. Two. Three. They let me go.

This Funny Life

1. Formative

The mother says look the houses are orange. Look you stupid idiot can't you see.
Now the houses are orange and you moron the mother says how can they be orange.
Now the houses aren't orange. And the mother is tired of talking. She leans over the
newspaper to fold it in half a half minute. Where are you where are you she screams
bustling into the kitchen. Comes into the corner searching for the child. Don't do that
again I can't take it.
Then the father comes in. He's wearing hockey pads. Where's my puck he says to the
mother.
God Christ you scared me says the mother.
Now the mother is quiet. And the father. And the child. Exhausted, all, by being
formed.
Puck fuck the child says asleep
But where is sleep the mother says.

2. Donner Party

The Donners were the ones who ate each other
now they're washing their socks.
Now the Donners are humming on the john.
Will they go out for Chinese or Japanese
the hand of the fish shaking its scalp?
Now the Donners are racing fast cars one flips over
but jumps up squealing. One girl starts to menstruate now the Donners are
snowboarding reversing so they go the other way pushing their cuticles down with an
orange stick the smell the long peel of orange.
Asking Is it over is it this

considerate skin?

The Robins Fly North

(after Flannery O'Connor)

The robins have flown back, stepping on board the 747, sinking into their seats, watching the jet throw its wings out, over Florida, over Miami Beach and the turbulent Everglades, pumping harder and harder to land with outstretched wheels on the cold grass of Providence.

Mr. Robin is still exhausted from lugging their luggage on and off the plane.

Any worms in the freezer? he yells.

Brian, you know I don't like you yelling things at me, says Mrs. Robin, trying to disentangle a nit from her leg.

What a filthy flight, she says, holding the nit up to the sun.

Where are the kids? says Mr. Robin.

What kids? says Mrs. Robin.

What kids? Our kids, Romulus and Remus, the ones you hatched. Wouldn't you like to see them after all this time?

Oh, God, sighs Mrs. Robin. Narrowing her eyes at the nit, she applies her beak to it like a disdainful hammer.

Airline food, she shudders.

I imagine they're where you left them, she says. In the nest with your mother.

Mr. Robin starts the harrowing climb up the tree. He hurt his foot on the beach the first day of the trip, on a broken beer bottle. Our kids aren't going to college, he promised his wife, furious to think some other parents' money was responsible for his cramped and bleeding claw. Some vacation, he thinks. Now he holds onto some twigs with his beak, trying to call out greetings as he pulls himself into the nest.

Mrrrderr! he says.

You could send a person a letter, yells his mother, fanning herself with one wing. You nearly gave me a heart attack.

What did you bring us? Romulus crowds past his grandmother and nearly knocks his father over. He's wearing an old housedress of hers, spattered with nasty droplets. Mr. Robin thinks he looks strange, alien, remarkably unkempt. Wait a minute, Son, he says, putting his wings out to keep Romulus back. Your old dad is in pain, give him a minute here!

Remus still has his eyes fixed on the TV screen.

Hi, Dad, he says. Grandma got drunk one night and passed out. He, too, looks strangely dressed. She fell on top of the TV and bent the antenna.

I did not! I fell asleep! You wore me out, morning to night!

Mr. Robin feels himself jolted, as always, by his mother's red breast inflating.

He applies his mouth to his claw, trying to fix the Band-Aid.

Mother, come over here please. After a long time she gets up from the recliner.

It is true what Remus tells me?

I had a fainting spell. He can see her beady eyes, shifting under the thick glasses.

What program were they watching?

Bird Man of Alcatraz.

Such trash! He remembers the nonsense about the deranged convict, holding innocent birds hostage in a cage. And anyway, I happen to know that was a midnight movie. What were they doing up at midnight?

We had a little party, she says primly. Leaving an old woman alone with two active boys! I wanted to spark myself up a little. The nasty twits!

Mother, your grandchildren, my sons! Mr. Robin takes his mouth from his claw.

Here, he says quickly. I brought you each back a nice big grapefruit. They grow them down there.

Romulus smirks at the pinkish globe.

A grapefruit! says Remus, not removing his eyes from the TV. Aw Dad, what am I supposed to do with this gross thing?

Do whatever you want! His father holds his wing to his head. Hey, where's all my whiskey! Mr. Robin is looking in the liquor cabinet. Mother, you drank every bit!

All of it, says Remus spitefully.

And why are you wearing your mother's bra, Remus? And why are the bird lice swimming freely along your eyelids?

This has not been Mr. Robin's day.

The old breast is nearly suffocating him, like an air bag.

Tell her she can have my old grapefruit, says Remus, tossing his away.

Mine too, says Romulus.

Mother, stop! Mr. Robin cries.

But she will not stop, lying face down on her red volcanic pillow, from smiling a little.

Or driving her beak, again and again, into the voluptuous and innocent grapefruits.

Saved

Unless you risk blaspheming nothing emerges. Like a bear poked in the yellow fat. Ask the Baptist for Coca-Cola, a slice of white bread. The Presbyter sips wine, but wishes he was Elvis.

It's a huge meal, the pork dark from its dangling, the matzoh cramped, solid as a bruise. Catching up with your mouth these just might enter. You think, Now if only it would open. Ow, ow ow, whines the Lord God. Next thing the cuticle bleeds, the Coke washes down and down. The lip chases, the palm quivers like it's touched. Somehow the mouth keeps crawling forward.

The lamb nuzzles outside, the sheep and the lion. The fluffy clouds that say our names. On the big pages Fluff and Sally leap for joy, in that book that falls to the floor when the teacher turns her back.

Susan Smith Nash

THREE STORIES

My Hair Shirt has Fleas

"You may not believe me. I know my son doesn't believe me. But, God has put me here and I can't leave until He lets me go."

I was talking to The Colonel, an ex-Air Force fighter pilot and Vietnam vet who was explaining to me that he was "God's Hostage" and was forbidden to leave the tiny motel room he had been renting now for eight years. The place was called "The Oasis" and it was owned by a nice Indian family who greeted customers from behind a bulletproof glass. If it was an oasis, the surrounding area had to be pretty bad. It was.

I wasn't listening to The Colonel, even though I should have been. It was research for the investigation I was doing on messianic delusions. I couldn't concentrate.

"I made myself a hair shirt out of old brushes and wool blankets. Do you want to see it?" asked The Colonel.

"Uh, sure," I said.

His story was pathetically familiar, although he believed himself unique. I tried to look politely interested as I watched the hot summer heat radiate up from the parking lot. A black man was unloading the trunk of his car.

Once, when my life was confusing, I decided that I, too, would try the monastic life. Looking back, I think I was intrigued by the adventure of it—a Dark Night of the Soul, that included flagellation with cat-o'-nine-tails, walking on my knees, and fasting.

"It's just your love of adventure," said my mother, dismissively.

That wasn't at all true. It was my attempt to understand myself. Unfortunately, I couldn't seem to arrive at self-understanding without self-destruction. I could be devilishly creative and marvelously persistent when it came to coming up with ways to undo, dissemble, and destroy myself.

"So. What you're doing is creating your own redemption in the form of a whip and a psychological lash," I said. "Am I right?"

He looked at me pityingly.

"Is that all you think?" he smirked. "Ha! You pathetic thing—I'm looking for liberation!"

What is liberation?

It was sounding suspiciously like death. Don't you remember the scene in *Double Indemnity* when Edward G. Robinson tells Fred MacMurray that when two co-conspirators hook up together on a murder/insurance scam they're committed—it's a one-way trip that ends at the cemetery.

I had been hoping for a new philosophy, an anti-machismo stance in which all the old war-bulls were hit with a huge dose of conscience and forced to spend their days writhing in misery for the emotional atrocities they had put their girlfriends and female significant others through.

But instead, it seemed that when faced with change, men on the edge turned to even more of the clichés of phallus-gun, go-Postal, settle-your-differences-with-an-AK-47.

Last week, a guy in Arizona took his three sons out into the mountains on a camping trip. Somewhere along the way, he decided they were possessed by the devil and he had to save them at all costs. This has a sadly predictable ending. He killed one. That was his way of chasing the devil out of his son. Then he decapitated the body.

I started thinking of the strange trip that brought me here to The Colonel's aluminum foil-lined motel room. Like an old typewriter ribbon, the road had stretched ahead, falsely linear, like a map or a narrative.

The Colonel brought out a strange coat-like draping that had about 3 dozen brushes on the inside.

"I strap it on real tight with duct tape," he explained proudly.

He didn't know I had my own hair shirt—in fact, I considered myself something of an expert in hair shirts.

I put on my own hair shirt late at night, while thinking about all the weird extremes people go to heal their pasts, wondering again what on earth my own past injuries were and why they tormented me so much. I like the way my own hair shirt scratched my breasts, and when it was hot, a thin stream of sweat would form in the curves. My sweat would dribble down my ribs and I would itch in a way that no amount of scratching could satisfy. If I drank a glass of wine, the hair shirt would shed tears and rub the image of my old next-door neighbor into my heart. The pain was exquisite—it made me think my life was worth living.

Maybe The Colonel's ratty old hair shirt would do that for him, too.

But mine has fleas. His has despair. For me, even one tiny flea adds too much and my nerves are flayed raw and ragged—I begin to beg for the end. I can't take it. What a shame —one flea can ruin everything. The flea is the mind playing tricks on me, making me superimpose a male mindset on my female reality. Language's forms still scream MALE MALE MALE, excluding me from every possibility of self-acceptance. Is that the truth or a convenient excuse? That question is my flea. You put fleas into your own hair shirt.

Why root out the pain by disowning language itself? Or symbol-systems—like the homicidal father in Arizona, projecting his fears onto his own son, then cutting off his head? They go too far. I go too far. Stop me. I can't stop myself.

Dependence imitates self-reliance. Independence imitates childishness.

Don't cut off my head. Just let me wear my own hair shirt. It's not a good one, since I don't know what the purpose of it is, or what I'm supposed to be able to do or control after I take it off. It's an unflattering shade of dogfur brown. I doubt I'll learn much at this.

The Colonel is saying in an obnoxious, arrogant voice, "God rearranged my teeth so I would have the Truth."

My hair shirt has fleas.

Coyote Tobacco Plant

A woman rakes leaves despite the fact that they are still falling—falling faster than she can rake—falling like thoughts, in fact—like wind burrowing false consciousness into the minds of trick-or-treaters, who have begun to think of their quotidian face-in-the-mirror as their true selves, and of their costume as a masquerade, an assumed self. The woman rakes leaves the color of clotted blood.

A mail carrier places a postcard of *Nicotiana attenuata* (Coyote Tobacco Plant) in a neighbor's box: "Hi. Having fun. Wish you were here."

Upstairs, down the street, a man is feeling chest pains after drinking his fourth cup of coffee. He worries that he has a heart condition. He doesn't realize that the indigestion he felt two months ago was a mild heart attack. What he has now is only heartburn.

A boy who lives in the corner house is giving his mother a fistful of weeds pulled from the creekbed that runs through an empty lot. They are sticky-haired and bad-smelling. The flowers are like miniature trumpets. "Thank you, honey, these are beautiful." She searches for a small vase. She hopes he doesn't make a habit of pulling up flowers. Her chrysanthemums have just started to bloom. The boy looks at her and feels suddenly very small and very alone—his first intimations of the existential condition of absolute solitude that he can neither articulate nor connect with an image—except perhaps to the image of a mother thanking him for his lovely gift as she crinkles her nose, worries the sticky places on her fingers, and talks to him with a distracted, vacant voice. He is starting to feel an aversion to flowers—at least flower-giving.

The woman has finished raking leaves and is starting to shovel them into 55-gallon low-density polyethylene bags. The wind is picking up. Soon the yard will be buried in leaves.

Wildcatter

I'm writing from a cabin in northern Vermont. I hope no one finds me. I'm not quite sure where I am, anyway.

I don't want anyone to know I'm here.

What happened? At least there are no oil and gas wells in Vermont, and nothing to disrupt the natural flow of filial affection. I was there when the whole thing came crashing in on itself.

And now I don't want anyone to find me.

It can be hell working for a family business.

The allegorical theme of our hassles couldn't be denied any longer. Fuck the world. Blow it up. Joseph Conrad's *The Secret Agent* had nothing on us. The family was a formula for psychic mayhem. My brother spent years on an impossible quest—he was convinced there was a giant oil field still hidden south of Slaughterville, Oklahoma in township 8 north - range 2 west. My father spent years trying to create a utopia. My mother spent the same time trying to sleep.

Now I'm in Vermont. This is not Oklahoma. Oklahoma is one continuous ghost town of dreams and polychromatic mirages slicked like film on the surface of a puddle of once-potable water.

Wildcatter: a person who engages in high-risk oil and gas exploration efforts by drilling in places far distant from established production in hopes of finding significant new reserves.

Wildcatter: An adrenaline junkie. A compulsive gambler. A dreamer. A visionary. A glutton for self-destruction.

My brother's obsession was also his way of saying he wasn't ready to see things the way they are. Someone needed to introduce him to post-impressionist painting. He saw a giant oil field just a few miles south and east of his farm. Good? Maybe. Problem was, it was covered by a town. And a quicksand & water moccasin-infested river. Just how did he plan to drill for oil in the middle of that? Put up a barge? Stretch his hide across the nearest sand bar & prop the rig up against his ass?

Probably.

It's dark now. I hate the whine of mosquitoes. I like the sound of water on rocks. Narragansett Stream flows into the Connecticut River near here. Would anyone guess I'd come here? I'm not sure I care any more. I'm gambling that no one will find me.

Our biggest investors, Heinrich Schliemann and his wife, were sitting in the back seat of my brother's white BMW. Heinrich's wife had confused a junkyard for an installation of *objets trouvés*. Marcel Duchamp and a row of washing machines called Maytag Ranch, after Cadillac Ranch just west of Amarillo. The old Maytags were lined up under a section line of Dutch Elm-diseased trees, not arranged according to color or model, but according to fractally significant clusters of Harvest Gold and Avocado Green.

A guy in overalls and a plaid shirt was approaching us.

"Can I help you?"

"Sir, have you been reading Georges Bataille?" I asked.

He looked at me and dug a wad of Red Man chewing tobacco out of a pouch and stuck it in his cheek.

"Technology is the ultimate intrusion," he said.

"Sale stickers are still semiotic equivalents of work & thus they chain our minds to the concept of work even as our bodies are free," I said.

"I think you'd best be careful what you say around here. That's for your own good." He spit a long stream of brown juice onto the Bermuda grass.

"What do you do with all these old Maytags?"

"I adjust their frequencies." He sat on the top of an avocado green one. "What do you mean?" I asked. "Each one has its own frequency of vibration. You sit on it & it will stimulate your own vibrations and you can get into the orgone-download realm." His accent became more southern as he got more Reichian.

"What kind of orgone energy can a Maytag accumulate?" I was incredulous. I would sit on my washing machine tonight while I did laundry.

"Metaphor actually introduces a subterranean communication, a movement of sympathy (or antipathy) which is its true *raison d'etre.*" (Alain Robbe-Grillet)

Investors driving up to the location. My brother, trying to convince himself of his geological authority. My dad, presenting the best-case possibility: "If we hit oil, if we offset, if we develop the field. . ." Me, making sure I don't wear my purple leather driving gloves, my Ray-Bans, my big fake-fur coat, Dalmatian-print boots. I wear jeans & cowboy boots instead. I pose myself under a billboard that could have been designed by Dali.

I was tired of investors dragging their dreams into my reality. Investors making a play for "mind-share"—that is, I had to start caring about their interests more than mine.

Maintain concentration, I reminded myself. It would be easier if I could wear a better disguise than anonymity.

Investors didn't want the small reservoirs—they didn't want to hear about 50 mcf per day of natural gas from a coalbed methane seam. They wanted 500 barrels a day from the first of many wells drilled in a field.

Frustration.

The nights are already cold in northern Vermont, even though it is still August. Rain in the afternoon, shrouds of fog in the morning. Fish embellish the ambience by jumping.

I'm hoping no one will figure out I've come here. If they know me, they'll think of coming here. It's obvious. My father's family owned this land for 8 generations. It's nothing to be proud of—it only keeps me rooted in the past—in my genetically determined capacity for mayhem and self-destruction.

Right.

The skies and the trees are just too unmanageable when they come in contact with the American myth of the eternal frontier. Streets paved with symbolism, and all that—

A white dove. A red hawk. An ant carrying six times its weight in food.

My dad had this little habit, you see. I called it Death Valley Days, after the television series sponsored by 20-mule team borax products. He called it "wildcatting." Others would call it "brave" or "visionary" or "courageous." The most pernicious compliment was the "making a contribution to the knowledge of our earth" line.

What would they say if they knew such a quest would rob him of his soul and condemn his children to the ledges of slippery, oozing suburbia he himself should have visited?

You might say I never believed in a soul anyway. It's reality that matters.

That was part of my "ethical and existential dilemma" (as I used to refer to it). There were ways around reality, and I was quite determined to find them. The man selling ice cream during January made his living hustling a concept—Preservation. Too bad it was only in the form of endless sleep, or a mound of ice and a frozen popsicle stick. Sleep was a wrapper of dreams to keep the thaw away. My arms felt wooden when I had to describe the latest prospect.

I never got used to it. Each time we plugged a well, I had a migraine attack.

"If your head hurts, take an aspirin!" My brother was a master of the cliché.

Don't stick an ice pick up your nostrils to cure a transitory pain. The predictable pain was like walking barefoot in the snow around a well about to be plugged and abandoned. After awhile, my toes were numb. Frostbite doesn't hurt if you're boiling your mind in Bataille.

Without humility, life treats skin like razors run over sandpaper. Ceremonies always seem to end the moment they begin. Is that what you might define as predictable. I'm not rigorous.

Outside the sky was working reds against the blues. Wheat was just turning yellow. Who could ever conceive of a happy, bright labyrinth? I remembered swimming in a pool and hearing meadowlarks. Scissortail flycatchers were perched on telephone lines. The sky was filled with invisible labyrinths. Minotaurs must have been in the clouds, not in the clear yellow light.

"No." I liked the blunt answer. It sounded more truthful, somehow, although I was merely groping for armor.

"What are you afraid of?" he asked.

I knew I'd better hang onto a good explanation as well as I could—as long as the quiet city meant relief from self, or a relief from the usual parade of revenge fantasies that played themselves out like worried neighbors peaking into windows and looking for signs of crime. My brother wanted me to make order from disorder. The oil wells would have to wait. They felt too much like death or warmed-over split-pea soup.

What the oil industry was really about was finding the ultimate division of property—who died? who profited? who got what? when? how much & for how long?—but what they really sought the ultimate sign—assurances of death in the form of blue flesh or shivering hair. Death and stasis signify the ultimate realm of order.

I was worried. One afternoon I became convinced my dreams had begun to go into someone else's body.

I dreamed I was in a department store when a car bomb went off. Doctors were extracting long slivers of glass from my abdomen and my eyes. I felt sharp ripping as they pulled against my gut. But then I saw my dreams slip into another person's body. Did the recipient of my dreams feel that pain? Was I responsible?

I did not will my nightmares away. They simply slipped out and did their damage in a random, uncontrollable way.

Is this what it means to get older, to lose your dreams?

About the Authors

LAURA MORIARTY'S recent books are *like roads* (Kelsey St. Press), *Rondeaux* (Roof Books), *L'Archiviste* (Zasterle Press) and *Symmetry* (Avec Books). *Symétrie*, selections from *Symmetry*, was published in French translation in 1997 by Editions Creaphis, Un Bureau sur l'Atlantique and The Foundation Royaumont. She received a Wallace Alexander Gerbode Foundation Award in Poetry in 1992. Her writing was recently chosen for *The Gertrude Stein Awards in Innovative American Poetry: 1996-1997*, forthcoming from Sun & Moon Press, and the *Moving Borders* anthology forthcoming from Talisman House. She lives in Albany, CA.

CHRIS STROFFOLINO'S books are *Cusps* and *Oops*. Forthcoming is *Light as a Fetter* from Situations Press. He lives and is underemployed in Brooklyn.

LAYNIE BROWNE'S books include *Hereditary Zones* (1993), *One Constellation* (1994), and forthcoming are *Rebecca Letters, Pollen Memory*, and *The Agency of Wind*. Her poems have appeared recently in *Rhizome*, and *The Gertrude Stein Awards In Innovative American Poetry*. Work is forthcoming in *Common Knowledge*, and in *re:* chapbook # 3. She lives in Seattle, Washington where she is one of the curators of the Subtext Reading Series.

GEORGE ALBON is the author of *Possible Floor* and *King*. His work has appeared in *Hambone, Ribot, Five Fingers Review*, AVEC and the *Gertrude Stein Awards in Innovative American Poetry*. He lives in San Francisco.

STEPHEN-PAUL MARTIN is the author of many books of fiction, poetry and nonfiction. His most recent collection of stories, *Not Quite Fiction*, was published by Vatic Hum Press in 1997. Other books of fiction include *Fear & Philosophy* (Detour Press, 1994) and *The Gothic Twilight* (Asylum Arts Press, 1992).

LISSA MCLAUGHLIN has written film reviews and a children's picture book. Her fiction has appeared in *The Massachusetts Review* and *The Best American Short Stories: 1982*. Her most recent collection of short prose is *Troubled by His Complexion* (Burning Deck, 1988). She lives in San Francisco with Lou Roberts, and is studying to be an art therapist.

SUSAN SMITH NASH received her Ph.D. in literature from the University of Oklahoma, where she teaches film and literature classes. Her latest book, *Channel-Surfing the Apocalypse*, is from Avec Books, and she has a book of plays, *Catfishes & Jackals*, forthcoming from Potes and Poets Press. Nash edits Texture Press, and is currently working on an anthology of Paraguayan women writers.

Hard Press Profile Series
Art & Literary Masterworks

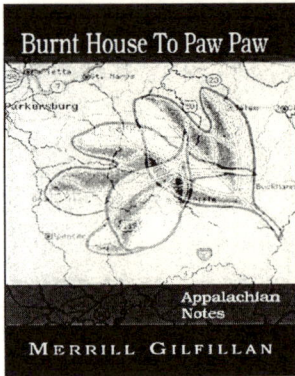

Burnt House to Paw Paw — *Merrill Gilfillan*

Gilfillan is the award-winning short story writer and poet whose *Magpie Rising: Sketches from the Great Plains,* won the first PEN/Martha Albrand award for non-fiction. In announcing the award, Donald Barthelme, Annie Dillard and Richard Gilman wrote: "*Magpie Rising* is clearly the work of a poet, both in the formal meaning of someone who writes verse and in the metaphorical designation of a quality of mind...As judges, we couldn't have wished for a worthier book with which to inaugurate this award."

Five years later, Gilfillan returns to the genre with a new collection of carefully crafted, deliberately developed pieces that grew from travels along the highways and back roads of the often alluded to, but rarely engaged, region of folklore known as "Appalachia."
$12.95, 132 ppm., ISBN 1-889097-05-5

Inventory: New and Selected Poems — *Frank Lima*
Edited and introduced by David Shapiro

When so much of the dross of the Sixties has fallen away, it is breathtaking to re-encounter the exemplary, tender, incandescent, incendiary, utterly authentic poems of Frank Lima. Reading them now, thirty years later, is like stumbling on the essential work of a lost American master—the missing piece of suffering and art that redeems the whole. What makes that discovery all the more startling is the more recent poetry, which shows Lima has been with us all along, continuing to write lyrical, imaginative poemas humanas. He has kept the faith; it is now our job to take in his accomplishment.

—Phillip Lopate

$12.95, 190 ppm., ISBN 1-889097-10-1

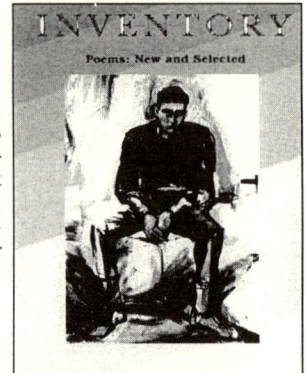

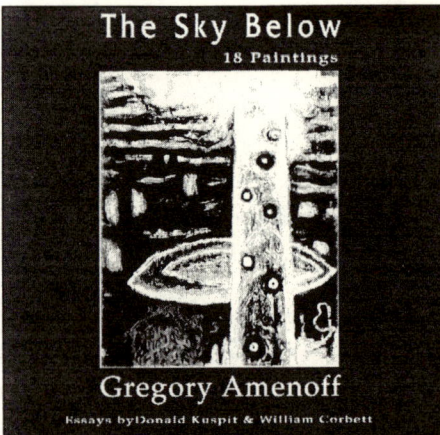

The Sky Below — *Gregory Amenoff*

Essays by William Corbett and Donald Kuspit.

Gregory Amenoff, who has been a recipient of three National Endowment for the Arts Awards and whose work has been shown and collected in galleries and museums internationally, has been heralded as "one of the best painters around" (Donald Kuspit, *Artforum*). Inspired by the poetry of William Blake, *The Sky Below* is comprised of visionary paintings that echo the work of Charles Burchfield and Martin Johnson Heade and that bring "the sky down to earth and ground starlight into pigment" (Bill Corbett). *The Sky Below*, includes 18 full-color reproductions of an exhibit currently on tour nationally.

$39.95, 48 ppm. 11 x 10, 18 full color reproductions, 5 drawings.

Order direct • Hard Press, Inc. • P. O. Box 184 • West Stockbridge, MA • 01266

1517